FINDING FACES IN THE CLOUDS:
A JUMP-START TO JOY

Daily Moments

By
KERRY MATSON

Thank you to my parents
for providing years
of laughter and countless
moments of joy.

THE JOURNEY TO JOY

Ok, it happened again. That guy cut you off in traffic this morning and the drive-thru girl got your order entirely wrong. You ended up with bacon when you asked for sausage. It's a disaster in the making! What about that person who stole your coveted parking spot, or the woman who didn't hold the elevator for you? Yes, your day is shaping up to be a bad one. You are now officially in a "mood."

Of course, these may not be your specific triggers, but I think you probably get the point. It really is interesting how many times we allow these types of small things to get us out of whack. The unfortunate ripple effect of what we deem to be big will usually end up directing our day. We need to change that.

If we can let those little frustrating experiences lead us in the wrong direction, we should be able to do the opposite. We should be able to find our joy in the small and the seemingly trivial things just as easily. However, sometimes we need a jump-start to get us going in the right direction.

This book certainly does not try to provide answers to life's biggest questions. Instead, it is meant to be a gentle, daily reminder for you to explore joy for yourself. These short daily thoughts are what help bring a smile to my face and get my day re-directed, if necessary. My hope is that they will do the same for you.

Yes, some are silly and some are very random indeed, and some are just plain ole "bucket list" items for me. All, however, have the purpose of getting your day started with a smile and a happy thought. One spark of joy, can lead to another and then another. Cultivate joyful thoughts. Ponder and practice them. Make it a habit and make them a choice.

As you read each daily moment, give yourself the green-light. Agree or disagree, but open your mind and allow these moments, these suggestions, to remind you of what it is that makes you smile. These are meant to be simple "joy-igniters" for you. I encourage you to come up with your own. Try it one day and one moment at a time. I think you'll be happily surprised.

January 1

A jump-start to joy is...

Being able to gain
a new perspective in life
by reading a nursery rhyme.

January 2

A jump-start to joy is...

Spinning a world globe,
and picking out the places
you would like to visit
in the future.

January 3

A jump-start to joy is...

Starting your New Year's diet
with a piece of cake in your hand.

January 4

A jump-start to joy is...

Remembering in the morning
the good dreams you
had the night before.

January 5

A jump-start to joy is...

Walking on the beach
and getting sand
between your toes.

January 6

A jump-start to joy is...

Being able to sleep in
while others are working.

January 7

A jump-start to joy is…

Finishing your workout
without injuring yourself.

January 8

A jump-start to joy is…

Having the same waist size
you had last year
and being ok with it.

January 9

A jump-start to joy is…

Enjoying the journey
as much as the destination.

January 10

A jump-start to joy is...

Stepping on the scales
and not exceeding the
maximum weight capacity

January 11

A jump-start to joy is...

Letting go of past mistakes and
concentrating on the triumphs ahead.

January 12

A jump-start to joy is...

Building a snowman and
burning calories in the process.

January 13

A jump-start to joy is...

Taking a tropical vacation
when it is cold and
snowy at home.

January 14

A jump-start to joy is...

Doing something you love to do,
even if you don't get paid for it.

January 15

A jump-start to joy is...

Attending a luau party and
learning how to Hula dance.

January 16

A jump-start to joy is...

Mouthing the words
to your favorite song
while working out.

January 17

A jump-start to joy is...

Listening to people
sing karaoke and not cringing.

January 18

A jump-start to joy is...

Concentrating on the positives
with negatives all around.

January 19

A jump-start to joy is…

Counting down the days
until your vacation begins.

January 20

A jump-start to joy is…

Going ice skating with friends.

January 21

A jump-start to joy is…

Stepping off the plane
to start your vacation.

January 22

A jump-start to joy is…

Starting a snowball fight.

January 23

A jump-start to joy is…

Singing in the shower
(in any key) at the top of your lungs.

January 24

A jump-start to joy is…

Having a great idea
and having someone else
agree with you that it is great.

January 25

A jump-start to joy is...

Napping on a snowy day.

January 26

A jump-start to joy is...

Rearranging the living room furniture
and not losing the TV remote.

January 27

A jump-start to joy is...

Creating an annual bucket list
and crossing items off
as you experience them.

January 28

A jump-start to joy is…

Setting a goal and sticking to it,
even when it would be
easier to give up.

January 29

A jump-start to joy is…

Being able to resist the donut
that is staring you in the eye.

January 30

A jump-start to joy is…

Finding a cause to believe in
and helping make a difference.

January 31

A jump-start to joy is…

Looking for ways to grow as a
person by getting to know
people from all walks of life.

February 1

A jump-start to joy is…

Having the courage to put
your life's dream into action,
even in the midst of naysayers.

February 2

A jump-start to joy is…

Sharing a "belly laugh" with a friend.

February 3

A jump-start to joy is…

Realizing it is not too late,
before it is too late.

February 4

A jump-start to joy is…

Taking that first dip into the
hotel pool after checking-in.

February 5

A jump-start to joy is…

Smiling at an attractive stranger
while grocery shopping.

February 6

A jump-start to joy is…

Hearing the Caribbean steel drums
being played as you board a cruise ship.

February 7

A jump-start to joy is…

Getting the call
that the office is closed
due to inclement weather.

February 8

A jump-start to joy is…

Browsing the sale items at your
favorite home "fix it" store.

February 9

A jump-start to joy is...

Taking the day off
to visit a museum.

February 10

A jump-start to joy is...

Watching a James Dean
movie marathon.

February 11

A jump-start to joy is...

Listening to the soft
purr of a cat.

February 12

A jump-start to joy is…

Cuddling. Period.

February 13

A jump-start to joy is…

Being tickled by
someone you love.

February 14

A jump-start to joy is…

Saying "I love you" and
receiving an
"I love you too" response.

February 15

A jump-start to joy is...

Going to an afternoon movie
during a snow storm.

February 16

A jump-start to joy is...

Getting your back scratched
or rubbed without having
to return the favor.

February 17

A jump-start to joy is...

Sitting by a ski lodge fireplace
and watching the snow fall.

February 18

A jump-start to joy is...

Attending a college basketball game.

February 19

A jump-start to joy is...

Going sled riding
while it is still snowing.

February 20

A jump-start to joy is...

Quoting lines from movies
with friends and trying to sound
like the characters.

February 21

A jump-start to joy is…

Packing for a tropical vacation.
Anytime and always.

February 22

A jump-start to joy is…

Perfecting the art
of people watching
at the airport.

February 23

A jump-start to joy is…

Being able to make a lot of money
and maintain the integrity
you had before you made it.

February 24

A jump-start to joy is…

Knowing where to turn,
when the GPS doesn't.

February 25

A jump-start to joy is…

Watching a classic
black and white movie.

February 26

A jump-start to joy is…

Holding a puppy.

February 27

A jump-start to joy is...

Splitting a donut
with a friend and
being ok with it.

February 28

A jump-start to joy is...

Treating others the
way you would
like to be treated.

February 29

A jump-start to joy is...

Skipping the chores for a day
and taking time to play.

March 1

A jump-start to joy is…

Dancing, even when
the music stops.

March 2

A jump-start to joy is…

Keeping track of your wins,
not your losses.

March 3

A jump-start to joy is…

Being on the beach
and hearing the
caw of sea gulls.

March 4

A jump-start to joy is…

Planning your next vacation,
while on vacation.

March 5

A jump-start to joy is…

Filling out your
brackets for the
March basketball tournaments.

March 6

A jump-start to joy is…

Receiving a big break
and paying it forward.

March 7

A jump-start to joy is…

Hiking the Na Pali coast
of Kauai, Hawaii.

March 8

A jump-start to joy is…

Taking a power nap
while on your lunch break.

March 9

A jump-start to joy is…

Making eye contact
with an attractive stranger
and feeling comfortable that
it isn't considered staring.

March 10

A jump-start to joy is…

Having a bowl
of homemade chili.

March 11

A jump-start to joy is…

Finding an inexpensive
Bloody Mary special.

March 12

A jump-start to joy is…

Riding the ferris wheel
at the Santa Monica Pier.

March 13

A jump-start to joy is...

Hearing your favorite
college team's fight song
being played.

March 14

A jump-start to joy is...

Going to the circus
and not being afraid
of the clowns.

March 15

A jump-start to joy is...

Spending the day at the
Metropolitan Museum of Art.

March 16

A jump-start to joy is…

Finding matching socks
after doing the laundry.

March 17

A jump-start to joy is…

Having breakfast with
friends at an Irish Pub.

March 18

A jump-start to joy is…

Making up a reason
to have a food day at work.

March 19

A jump-start to joy is...

Seeing the sun come up
over the ocean's horizon.

March 20

A jump-start to joy is...

Volunteering to help
someone who needs it.

March 21

A jump-start to joy is...

Going to a spring training
baseball game.

SPRING

It is finally here!
Out with the old
and in with the new.

As you continue to cultivate your
journey to joy, be intentional.

Purposefully be aware of
the new growth and
the blossoming potential
that is all around you.

*What little things can you be doing
this Spring that will help your joy grow?*

March 22

A jump-start to joy is…

Having scrambled eggs
and pancakes for dinner.

March 23

A jump-start to joy is…

Being happy that your DVR
didn't cut the ending off
of your favorite show.

March 24

A jump-start to joy is…

Spreading compliments,
not rumors.

March 25

A jump-start to joy is…

Hitting the snooze button
and not being late for work.

March 26

A jump-start to joy is…

Waking up to the
sound of ocean waves.

March 27

A jump-start to joy is…

Expanding your comfort zone
by trying something new.

March 28

A jump-start to joy is…

Finding a twenty dollar bill
in your jeans pocket
after washing them.

March 29

A jump-start to joy is…

Hunting for Easter eggs
and letting someone else
win the hunt.

March 30

A jump-start to joy is…

Giving of your time to someone,
even if you don't have the time.

March 31

A jump-start to joy is…

Being able to use
frequent flyer points
for a vacation trip.

April 1

A jump-start to joy is…

Having fun like a fool,
but not actually being one.

April 2

A jump-start to joy is…

Going for a run in the rain.

April 3

A jump-start to joy is...

Enjoying the first warm day
of Spring after a long, cold winter.

April 4

A jump-start to joy is...

Being able to go
to the home opener to watch
your favorite baseball team play.

April 5

A jump-start to joy is...

Singing "Take Me Out to the Ballgame"
during the seventh inning stretch.

April 6

A jump-start to joy is…

Hearing a toddler
begin to formulate words.

April 7

A jump-start to joy is…

Picking a bouquet
of Lilacs for your living room.

April 8

A jump-start to joy is…

Playing fetch with your dog.

April 9

A jump-start to joy is...

Writing management about the
great service you received,
not the opposite.

April 10

A jump-start to joy is...

Hearing the sound
of thunder from an
approaching storm.

April 11

A jump-start to joy is...

Watching a kitten
and puppy play together.

April 12

A jump-start to joy is...

Being able to leave
work on time.

April 13

A jump-start to joy is...

Getting a kite
to actually take flight.

April 14

A jump-start to joy is...

Eating a lunch on a picnic blanket
while basking in the spring sun.

April 15

A jump-start to joy is...

Walking through a Botanical Garden
and taking in all the beauty.

April 16

A jump-start to joy is...

Making something for
someone, instead of, buying it.

April 17

A jump-start to joy is...

Waking up to the sound
of birds chirping.

April 18

A jump-start to joy is...

Taking your dog
for a walk.

April 19

A jump-start to joy is...

Driving around with
the sunroof open,
even when it is raining.

April 20

A jump-start to joy is...

Having your favorite
fountain drink.

April 21

A jump-start to joy is...

Picking fresh flowers
for your dining room table.

April 22

A jump-start to joy is...

Re-Reading your favorite book.

April 23

A jump-start to joy is...

Seeing tulips begin to bloom.

April 24

A jump-start to joy is…

Hearing the croak of
frogs after a spring rain.

April 25

A jump-start to joy is…

Making a positive difference
in someone's day.

April 26

A jump-start to joy is…

Waking up to
the smell of coffee.

April 27

A jump-start to joy is…

Going to a parade
(of any kind) in New York.

April 28

A jump-start to joy is…

Being able to bite your tongue
to keep from saying that one thing
you would later regret.

April 29

A jump-start to joy is…

Stomping in rain puddles
and not caring that your
shoes are getting wet.

April 30

A jump-start to joy is…

Browsing through
dollar store items.

May 1

A jump-start to joy is…

Going to an auction.

May 2

A jump-start to joy is…

Being able to
laugh at yourself.

May 3

A jump-start to joy is...

Seeing how excited your dog
gets when you say the word "treat."

May 4

A jump-start to joy is...

Planting your first
flower of the spring.

May 5

A jump-start to joy is...

Having chips and salsa
at your favorite
Mexican restaurant.

May 6

A jump-start to joy is…

Knowing the correct path
to take when there are
multiple forks in the road.

May 7

A jump-start to joy is…

Holding hands with the
person you love.

May 8

A jump-start to joy is…

Sitting on the patio and
reading the morning headlines.

May 9

A jump-start to joy is…

Smelling the scent
of a rain in the air.

May 10

A jump-start to joy is…

Getting your passport stamped.

May 11

A jump-start to joy is…

Watching a child play tee ball.

May 12

A jump-start to joy is…

Seeing a Broadway show.

May 13

A jump-start to joy is…

Sitting on a park bench
and feeding the pigeons.

May 14

A jump-start to joy is…

Going for a bike ride
with friends.

May 15

A jump-start to joy is...

Finding a restroom
"just in time" while on a road trip.

May 16

A jump-start to joy is...

Having someone else
mow your lawn.

May 17

A jump-start to joy is...

Walking on the wave wall
of Ft. Lauderdale Beach.

May 18

A jump-start to joy is…

Having your Girl Scout cookie
purchases finally arrive.

May 19

A jump-start to joy is…

Getting a deep tissue massage
from a world class spa.

May 20

A jump-start to joy is…

Hearing a chorus of moos
from a herd of cattle.

May 21

A jump-start to joy is…

Watching a dog
chase ocean waves.

May 22

A jump-start to joy is…

Finding a great taco special.

May 23

A jump-start to joy is…

Taking a peaceful walk
in the countryside.

May 24

A jump-start to joy is…

Laying in bed listening
to the thunder and rain.

May 25

A jump-start to joy is…

Riding a jet ski
and jumping the waves.

May 26

A jump-start to joy is…

Getting a pay increase
without getting
increased responsibilities.

May 27

A jump-start to joy is…

Having good friends
who get your "quirkiness"
and love you anyway.

May 28

A jump-start to joy is…

Hearing the sound
of slot machines
in a Las Vegas casino.

May 29

A jump-start to joy is…

Remembering fondly the good times
you have had with loved ones.

May 30

A jump-start to joy is…

Watching a fireworks show
and listening to patriotic music.

May 31

A jump-start to joy is…

Screaming on a roller coaster
and not being embarrassed
about your shriek.

June 1

A jump-start to joy is…

Touring a vineyard
and sampling the wines.

June 2

A jump-start to joy is…

Playing in a summer softball league.

June 3

A jump-start to joy is…

Having it still be
daylight at 8pm.

June 4

A jump-start to joy is…

Playing travel bingo
on a road trip.

June 5

A jump-start to joy is...

Finding faces in the clouds.

June 6

A jump-start to joy is...

Playing in the
lawn water sprinklers.

June 7

A jump-start to joy is...

Browsing through
random items found
at a truck stop store.

June 8

A jump-start to joy is…

Listening to the sound
of crickets chirping at night.

June 9

A jump-start to joy is…

Buying fresh flowers
and vegetables at
the farmer's market.

June 10

A jump-start to joy is…

Visiting Hoover Dam
and taking in the
view of Lake Mead.

June 11

A jump-start to joy is…

Offering compassion to people,
not indifference.

June 12

A jump-start to joy is…

Sitting on a beach
and just listening to
the sounds around you.

June 13

A jump-start to joy is…

Saying "thank you"
and really meaning it.

June 14

A jump-start to joy is…

Experiencing the
Pike Place fish market
in Seattle.

June 15

A jump-start to joy is…

Hearing the soft whistle
of a train in the distance.

June 16

A jump-start to joy is…

Skipping a rock across
a lake and counting
the number of skips.

June 17

A jump-start to joy is…

Getting away from
the city lights to look
for the Big Dipper.

June 18

A jump-start to joy is…

Hearing ballpark vendors
sell hot dogs and beer.

June 19

A jump-start to joy is…

Being fed breakfast in bed.

June 20

A jump-start to joy is…

Picnicking along
a mountain stream.

June 21

A jump-start to joy is…

Finding the right amount
of change for
the vending machine.

June 22

A jump-start to joy is…

Buying a hot dog or brat
from a food truck.

SUMMER

Ah, the joys of Summer.
Baseball games, pool parties,
the 4th of July, and homemade ice cream are all
flavors of the season.

As you experience the sunny months ahead,
make it a goal to create your own recipe of fun.

*What simple and everyday ingredients can
you include to fill your Summer with joy?*

June 23

A jump-start to joy is…

Finding a clean restroom
in a National Park.

June 24

A jump-start to joy is…

Hearing the crack
of the bat
at a baseball game.

June 25

A jump-start to joy is…

Playing sand volleyball
with friends.

June 26

A jump-start to joy is...

Staying up late
to chase lightening bugs
around the yard.

June 27

A jump-start to joy is...

Taking a white water rafting
trip in Colorado.

June 28

A jump-start to joy is...

Taking a boat tour
of Niagara Falls
and feeling the spray
gently hit your face.

June 29

A jump-start to joy is…

Counting the number
of plane trails you can see
in a clear blue sky.

June 30

A jump-start to joy is…

Eating mom's homemade
fried chicken.

July 1

A jump-start to joy is…

Hearing the ringing bell
and music of
an ice cream truck.

July 2

A jump-start to joy is…

Being able to still play
recess games as an adult.

July 3

A jump-start to joy is…

Finding bargains
at a garage sale.

July 4

A jump-start to joy is…

Shooting off fireworks
without getting injured
or burning the house down.

July 5

A jump-start to joy is...

Watching Saturday morning cartoons.

July 6

A jump-start to joy is...

Spending the day
at a water park.

July 7

A jump-start to joy is...

Swimming with dolphins
in the Caribbean.

July 8

A jump-start to joy is…

Taking a surfing class while
on vacation in Los Cabos.

July 9

A jump-start to joy is…

Finding something to heartily
laugh about every morning.

July 10

A jump-start to joy is…

Relaxing on a patio deck
with an appetizer and
a martini in hand.

July 11

A jump-start to joy is…

Making homemade ice cream.

July 12

A jump-start to joy is…

Blowing out birthday candles
and not catching
anything on fire.

July 13

A jump-start to joy is…

Running a 5k and not being
concerned what place you finished,
but happy *that* you finished.

July 14

A jump-start to joy is...

Making wishes
on shooting stars.

July 15

A jump-start to joy is...

Sitting under a shade tree
and drinking an iced tea.

July 16

A jump-start to joy is...

Starting a water balloon
fight with willing participants.

July 17

A jump-start to joy is…

Making "cannonball" splashes
in a swimming pool.

July 18

A jump-start to joy is…

Taking an afternoon nap
in a hammock.

July 19

A jump-start to joy is…

Smiling at someone
you don't know.

July 20

A jump-start to joy is...

Re-visiting your
New Year's resolutions
and realizing you've
made progress.

July 21

A jump-start to joy is...

Meeting someone special
for lunch.

July 22

A jump-start to joy is...

Playing "Wiffle Ball" and
pretending to be a major leaguer.

July 23

A jump-start to joy is…

Being there for a friend in need and
and knowing they would
do the same for you.

July 24

A jump-start to joy is…

Sweating the hot stuff,
not the small.

July 25

A jump-start to joy is…

Singing carols to celebrate
Christmas in July.

July 26

A jump-start to joy is…

Going to a drive-in theatre
and listening to the movie
through the radio.

July 27

A jump-start to joy is…

Eating cotton candy
at the ballpark.

July 28

A jump-start to joy is…

Reading a book
by the pool.

July 29

A jump-start to joy is…

Being able to
pay off or pay down
a credit card.

July 30

A jump-start to joy is…

Camping in your backyard
and pretending that
you are roughing it.

July 31

A jump-start to joy is…

Watching a little league
baseball game.

August 1

A jump-start to joy is...

Finding your smart phone
without destroying the house
while looking for it.

August 2

A jump-start to joy is...

Hearing the buzz of
locusts during the
dog days of summer.

August 3

A jump-start to joy is...

Laying on a blanket
under the night sky.

August 4

A jump-start to joy is…

Eating a freshly
picked watermelon.

August 5

A jump-start to joy is…

Catching up with
a good friend.

August 6

A jump-start to joy is…

Watching the sunset
over a corn field.

August 7

A jump-start to joy is…

Driving cross country
on Route 66.

August 8

A jump-start to joy is…

Getting your face
licked by a puppy.

August 9

A jump-start to joy is…

Taking a tour of a lighthouse.

August 10

A jump-start to joy is…

Laughing so hard
that you cry a little.

August 11

A jump-start to joy is…

Having fish and chips
at your favorite
seaside restaurant.

August 12

A jump-start to joy is…

Surprising the person
you love with
a birthday trip.

August 13

A jump-start to joy is…

Moisturizing before it
becomes a wrinkle.

August 14

A jump-start to joy is…

Having every light
be green on your
drive to work.

August 15

A jump-start to joy is…

Leaving work on
a Friday afternoon
to start your weekend.

August 16

A jump-start to joy is…

Receiving a "warning"
instead of an
actual traffic ticket.

August 17

A jump-start to joy is…

Being able to have an open mind
as well as an open heart.

August 18

A jump-start to joy is…

Going to the state fair
and playing carnival games.

August 19

A jump-start to joy is...

Looking through
old family photos.

August 20

A jump-start to joy is...

Hiking a mountain trail
to a secluded lake or waterfall.

August 21

A jump-start to joy is...

Taking a walk
with someone you love
and chatting about
nothing, but everything.

August 22

A jump-start to joy is…

Eating at your
favorite BBQ restaurant.

August 23

A jump-start to joy is…

Skating under
the limbo stick and
not hurting yourself.

August 24

A jump-start to joy is…

Becoming better in life,
not bitter.

August 25

A jump-start to joy is…

Learning to play nice
with challenging people.

August 26

A jump-start to joy is…

Holding a newborn baby.

August 27

A jump-start to joy is…

Receiving a compliment
about your new haircut.

August 28

A jump-start to joy is...

Rocking a baby to sleep.

August 29

A jump-start to joy is...

Drinking a glass of wine
while doing the laundry.

August 30

A jump-start to joy is...

Listening to classical music
with your car windows
rolled down.

August 31

A jump-start to joy is…

Singing to the song
on the radio.

September 1

A jump-start to joy is…

Playing free-style
croquet with
family and friends.

September 2

A jump-start to joy is…

Camping at the base
of Mt St Helens
and climbing it the next day.

September 3

A jump-start to joy is...

Reading a nursery rhyme to a child.

September 4

A jump-start to joy is...

Knowing who God is
and being okay
that it isn't you.

September 5

A jump-start to joy is...

Seeing the view of New York
from the top of
the Empire State Building.

September 6

A jump-start to joy is...

Taking a hot air balloon ride.

September 7

A jump-start to joy is...

Counting the number of
boxcars as you wait
for the train to pass.

September 8

A jump-start to joy is...

Listening to the
"Grand Ole Opry"
on the radio.

September 9

A jump-start to joy is…

Having a picnic
at the zoo.

September 10

A jump-start to joy is…

Watching a toddler
take their first steps.

September 11

A jump-start to joy is…

Planning a trip to visit
Sea World in San Diego.

September 12

A jump-start to joy is…

Doing something nice
for someone without
them knowing it.

September 13

A jump-start to joy is…

Eating kettle corn
and funnel cakes
at fall festivals.

September 14

A jump-start to joy is…

Cooking dinner
and having someone else
do the clean-up.

September 15

A jump-start to joy is…

Allowing yourself to be silly
and enjoying the experience.

September 16

A jump-start to joy is…

Sleeping in your own bed
after a long business trip.

September 17

A jump-start to joy is…

Paying for the person behind you
in the drive-thru line.

September 18

A jump-start to joy is…

Running *with* your dog,
not *after.*

September 19

A jump-start to joy is…

Celebrating "National Talk Like a Pirate Day"
by talking like one.

September 20

A jump-start to joy is…

Being able to laugh at pictures
of your old hairstyles.

September 21

A jump-start to joy is…

Going shopping at
antique stores with a friend.

September 22

A jump-start to joy is…

Remembering where you
placed your keys.

September 23

A jump-start to joy is…

Spending the day
with someone special.

AUTUMN

Funnel cakes, apple cider and
Fall festivals are everywhere this time of year.

As you transition from shorts to sweaters,
don't look at this season as an ending,
but as a beginning of an exciting, new way
to view the colors of the world around you.

*What are some ways that you are
actively seeking joy in the midst of change?*

September 24

A jump-start to joy is…

Knowing that you
aren't perfect and
accepting that fact.

September 25

A jump-start to joy is…

Showing kindness to someone
who really needs a dose of it.

September 26

A jump-start to joy is…

Trying out a new restaurant.

September 27

A jump-start to joy is...

Going bowling and
getting a "turkey."

September 28

A jump-start to joy is...

Taking the time to notice
the changing colors of the trees.

September 29

A jump-start to joy is...

Being in the speedy check-out line
and having it actually be speedy.

September 30

A jump-start to joy is...

Seeing a show at
an outdoor theatre.

October 1

A jump-start to joy is...

Finding loose change in
the sofa cushions.

October 2

A jump-start to joy is...

Putting out the
Halloween decorations.

October 3

A jump-start to joy is…

Being able to eat
whatever you want
on your birthday.

October 4

A jump-start to joy is…

Shopping for you Fall wardrobe.

October 5

A jump-start to joy is…

Sitting on your patio and
listening to music with
a glass of wine nearby.

October 6

A jump-start to joy is…

Browsing through
garage sale items.

October 7

A jump-start to joy is…

Taking a bike ride
and enjoying the fall foliage.

October 8

A jump-start to joy is…

Forgiving someone who
doesn't deserve it.

October 9

A jump-start to joy is...

Jumping in a pile
of freshly raked leaves.

October 10

A jump-start to joy is...

Cooking brats and
burgers on the grill.

October 11

A jump-start to joy is...

Being comfortable
with who you are
and being loved
for that very reason.

October 12

A jump-start to joy is…

Taking a train ride
to an Octoberfest celebration.

October 13

A jump-start to joy is…

Adopting a pet
from an animal shelter.

October 14

A jump-start to joy is…

Eating sunflower seeds
while watching the World Series.

October 15

A jump-start to joy is…

Dancing to 80's music
while cleaning the house.

October 16

A jump-start to joy is…

Going on a Sunday drive
with your family.

October 17

A jump-start to joy is…

Taking a painting class.

October 18

A jump-start to joy is...

Visiting a National Park.

October 19

A jump-start to joy is...

Coloring outside the lines,
even as an adult.

October 20

A jump-start to joy is...

Attending a Friday night
high school football game.

October 21

A jump-start to joy is...

Getting lost in
a corn maze with
someone special.

October 22

A jump-start to joy is...

Buying mums
for your front porch.

October 23

A jump-start to joy is...

Walking through
a pumpkin patch.

October 24

A jump-start to joy is…

Drinking hot apple cider
as you shop for
the perfect pumpkin.

October 25

A jump-start to joy is…

Bobbing for apples.

October 26

A jump-start to joy is…

Finding the perfect costume
for a Halloween party.

October 27

A jump-start to joy is…

Carving a Jack-O-Lantern.

October 28

A jump-start to joy is…

Seeing a full moon
low on the horizon.

October 29

A jump-start to joy is…

Being able to watch
a scary movie
with the lights off.

October 30

A jump-start to joy is...

Roasting marshmallows
over a camp fire.

October 31

A jump-start to joy is...

Going to haunted houses
with friends.

November 1

A jump-start to joy is...

Seeing a good friend
you haven't seen in awhile
and having it not seem that way.

November 2

A jump-start to joy is…

Getting an extra hour
of sleep because of
Daylight's Savings Time.

November 3

A jump-start to joy is…

Teaching yourself how
to play the guitar.

November 4

A jump-start to joy is…

Remembering the passwords
to all of your online accounts.

November 5

A jump-start to joy is...

Knowing that you won't have
to see more campaign ads
now that the elections are over.

November 6

A jump-start to joy is...

Having a bag of popcorn
all to yourself as you watch
your favorite TV show.

November 7

A jump-start to joy is...

Wearing your bowling shoes
and feeling fashionable.

November 8

A jump-start to joy is...

Taking pictures of trees
as the season changes.

November 9

A jump-start to joy is...

Surprising someone special
with a weekend getaway trip.

November 10

A jump-start to joy is...

Eating a box off thin mints
with a glass of milk.

November 11

A jump-start to joy is…

Cleaning your closets
and donating the clothes.

November 12

A jump-start to joy is…

Making a wish
before blowing out
your birthday candles.

November 13

A jump-start to joy is…

Going to a movie
on a school night.

November 14

A jump-start to joy is…

Having pumpkin pie
with whipped cream.

November 15

A jump-start to joy is…

Going home for the Holidays.

November 16

A jump-start to joy is…

Hearing the words "I love you"
from someone you
want to hear say them.

November 17

A jump-start to joy is…

Receiving birthday wishes from
your "Facebook Friends" and
actually knowing most of them.

November 18

A jump-start to joy is…

Being done with both
the laundry and the cleaning.

November 19

A jump-start to joy is…

Receiving a compliment
about your hair
when you thought
it was a bad hair day.

November 20

A jump-start to joy is…

Watching the
Thanksgiving Day Parade.

November 21

A jump-start to joy is…

Having your first
peppermint latte
of the season.

November 22

A jump-start to joy is…

Shopping in the afternoon
of Black Friday,
while everyone else
is at home napping.

November 23

A jump-start to joy is…

Being more thankful
for the *people* you have in life,
than the *things* you have.

November 24

A jump-start to joy is…

Playing board games
with family on holidays.

November 25

A jump-start to joy is…

Making a wish with
the turkey wishbone.

November 26

A jump-start to joy is…

Seeing the Christmas lights
of the Country Club Plaza
in Kansas City, Missouri.

November 27

A jump-start to joy is…

Waking up to the smell
of the turkey baking
on Thanksgiving morning.

November 28

A jump-start to joy is…

Napping on Thanksgiving Day.

November 29

A jump-start to joy is…

Creating new family traditions
while keeping the old.

November 30

A jump-start to joy is…

Hearing that Santa
has safely arrived
at the mall.

December 1

A jump-start to joy is…

Watching the classic
animated holiday TV specials.

December 2

A jump-start to joy is...

Putting up the
Christmas decorations.

December 3

A jump-start to joy is...

Going ice skating at
Rockefeller Center.

December 4

A jump-start to joy is...

Hearing that you have
made Santa's nice list.

December 5

A jump-start to joy is…

Shopping for and decorating
a Christmas tree.

December 6

A jump-start to joy is…

Receiving your first
Christmas card
of the season.

December 7

A jump-start to joy is…

Going to an ugly
Christmas sweater party.

December 8

A jump-start to joy is...

Buying the first item
on your Christmas list.

December 9

A jump-start to joy is...

Hearing the ring
of the Salvation Army Bells.

December 10

A jump-start to joy is...

Drinking a Pumpkin spice latte
while Christmas shopping.

December 11

A jump-start to joy is...

Finding new recipes
for the holiday dinners.

December 12

A jump-start to joy is...

Hearing a child sing
a Christmas carol.

December 13

A jump-start to joy is...

Watching it
begin to snow.

December 14

A jump-start to joy is…

Being able to remember
where you parked
after a day of shopping.

December 15

A jump-start to joy is…

Bundling up in a blanket
and watching your favorite
holiday movie.

December 16

A jump-start to joy is…

Buying the Christmas ham.

December 17

A jump-start to joy is...

Making it through
the holiday gatherings
without losing your
mind or your temper.

December 18

A jump-start to joy is...

Listening to
Christmas carolers
at a shopping mall.

December 19

A jump-start to joy is...

Being kissed under
the mistletoe by
your secret crush.

December 20

A jump-start to joy is...

Baking Christmas cookies
and eating the dough as you go.

December 21

A jump-start to joy is...

Watching "It's a Wonderful Life."

December 22

A jump-start to joy is...

Buying the last item
on your Christmas list.

WINTER

The season of giving and
the season of joy is upon us!

As you celebrate the Holidays
with carols and candles,
begin looking for fresh perspectives
for your upcoming New Year.

Experience the joy of the season
and the hope that it can bring.

*How can you maintain your joy while
going through the hustle and bustle
of the holiday season?*

December 23

A jump-start to joy is…

Seeing someone special
open up their
Christmas gifts.

December 24

A jump-start to joy is…

Singing "Silent Night"
at a Christmas eve service.

December 25

A jump-start to joy is…

Being with loved ones
on Christmas day.

December 26

A jump-start to joy is…

Having a champagne toast
to celebrate the holidays.

December 27

A jump-start to joy is…

Hitting up the clearance rack
at your favorite store.

December 28

A jump-start to joy is…

Having popcorn
with extra butter
before starting
your New Year's diet.

December 29

A jump-start to joy is...

Watching the ball drop
on New Year's eve.

December 30

A jump-start to joy is...

Being kissed by
someone you love
at midnight on
New Year's Eve.

December 31

A jump-start to joy is...

Knowing that tomorrow
you will have second chances
and a clean slate ahead of you.

2777920R00077

Made in the USA
San Bernardino, CA
03 June 2013